PRAYERABLES

PRAYERABLES

MEDITATIONS OF A HOMEMAKER

by Irene B. Harrell

WORD BOOKS  WACO, TEXAS

Many Scriptures quoted in this book are from the *Revised Standard Version of the Bible,* copyright 1946 and 1952 by the Division of Christian Education of the National Council of Churches.

FOREWORD

In his wonderful *Imitation of Christ* Thomas à Kempis observes, "If only your heart were right, then every created thing would be to you a mirror of life and a book of holy teaching."

And so I find it for myself. Days when my heart is right, days when my heart and mind are set on seeking first the kingdom of heaven, I find eternal truths and helpful insights for living in the most ordinary events of the day. It is, on such days, as if everything translates itself into a parable, understandable on other levels than the mere facts themselves.

I call these insights "Prayerables," because prayer is the natural culmination of our every experience—when our hearts are right. In sharing my "Prayerables" with you I hope to set you to seeking and finding, to the end that you might be more aware of the presence of God in your life.

PRAYERABLES

MEDITATIONS OF A HOMEMAKER

Fathers, do not provoke your children to anger, but bring them up in the discipline and instruction of the Lord. Ephesians 6:4 (RSV)

Since we moved into our new house I've been careful to buy only the mildest kind of scouring powder. I had read, somewhere, that while harsh, gritty powders will get the sink or bathtub clean in a hurry, they will leave scratches. The scratches make perfect places for dirt and germs to lodge, making the fixtures harder and harder to keep clean as time goes on.

A mild powder, on the other hand, takes a little longer to use and requires more effort in the application. But it doesn't scratch the porcelain. Fixtures carefully cleaned will still be gleaming and easy to care for years later.

Dear Lord, You have blessed me with beautiful children to love and to care for. Forgive me for the times when I have disciplined them harshly and unlovingly, with loud and angry scoldings. I know this kind of discipline has produced a surface obedience, but has left scars and scratches on the lovely nature of my children, rendering them more susceptible to the bad influences of the world. Let me discipline them with care and gentleness, that the loveliness they have from You will not be corrupted by my action. Amen.

3

If we confess our sins, he is faithful and just, and will forgive our sins and cleanse us from all unrighteousness. 1 John 1:9 (RSV)

My TEN YEAR OLD daughter had written a letter to her grandmother. She gave it to me to read before tucking it into an envelope to give to the postman. I had to chuckle out loud when I came to the sentence where Alice told grandmother what she had been doing on that particular rainy day. She had written, "I have been reading, sulking and sewing."

When Alice heard my outburst she knew what had made me laugh. She blushed a little bit as she looked at the rug and explained, "Well, I didn't want it to be a dull letter."

I thought of the dull letters I had written or received in the past—letters that would have been more interesting if I and my correspondents had been honest enough to tell of our short-comings and our failures. The whole truth is seldom dull, I thought, although our own protective siftings of it are frequently quite tedious.

My Lord, help me toward honesty in my prayers. Let me confess to You all my wrongdoing, that I may receive Your healing forgiveness in all things. For Jesus' sake. AMEN.

5

Where is he who has been born king of the Jews? For we have seen his star in the East, and have come to worship him. Matthew 2:2 (RSV)

I WAS SLICING APPLES for some cinnamon-apple rings when I noticed the almost perfect star formed by the pattern of the seeds in the fruit. To me, it was a special reminder of the Star of Bethlehem, which pointed the Wise Men to the place where the young Child lay. It was a kitchen reminder of the direction in which I should point my life.

Since that day I have looked for and found stars everywhere—in the seed patterns, blossom ends and leaf arrangements of pears, oranges, pine cones, roses, sunflowers, strawberries, squash, celery—even in the star within a star within a star folded in the heart of the lowly cabbage. These stars are vital to the life or heart of the fruit or flower or vegetable.

Heavenly Father, I thank You that You have planted the Star of the heavens in the fruit of the field to help me keep Him in my heart. Let me ever be mindful of You in the beautiful patterns of Your continuing creation. AMEN.

4

Put on the whole armor of God, that you may be able to stand against the wiles of the devil. Ephesians 6:11 (RSV)

I WAS OUTSIDE, attired for soaking up the summer sun, when I discovered to my surprise and delight that the blackberries were ripe in the field below our house. Eager to pick the first batch for a pie for supper I ran to the house for a basket and returned to the briars. Gingerly, to avoid being scratched, I reached slowly and carefully, picking what berries I could reach around the edges of the patch. I had to bypass the places where I could see berries hanging large and luscious, just out of reach. The few berries I got were small, seedy, fringe berries, painfully acquired.

The next day, in overalls, a heavy, long-sleeved shirt and high boots I headed for the blackberry patch. Without fear of being scratched I tramped boldly in to where the finest berries waited for me. In almost no time my basket was full and I hadn't been scratched a single time.

Dear Lord, living is like blackberry picking. Forgive me when, unsuitably attired, I reap a poor harvest, slowly and painfully. Let me put on the "whole armor of God" and partake of Your abundance, without worry or stumbling, without fear that the path will close behind me. I know that You will always provide the way I can trust. AMEN.   **9**

We know that in everything God works for good with those who love him, who are called according to his purpose. Romans 8:28 (RSV)

"WHAT A WASTE!" Our dinner guest surveyed the Thanksgiving table. What had been a beautiful array of plump, brown, roast turkey, mounds of snowy mashed potatoes, shimmering bowls of ruby cranberry sauce, neatly arranged piles of green asparagus, baskets of steaming rolls and trim squares of butter had been devastated. All the work and artistry lavished upon the preparation of a delicious meal seemed to have been transformed, by some black magic, into crumpled napkins, a mutilated turkey carcass, a half-empty bowl of dressing, a dozen plates streaked with gravy and almost as many over-stuffed stomachs. "It wasn't worth it!" he thought.

But our guest was shortsighted. He didn't know what I planned to do with the tragic debris. He didn't see the turkey sandwiches for lunch tomorrow, the delicious hash the day after, and the turkey soup put in the freezer. He didn't know about the frozen left-overs that would bring happy reminiscences of Thanksgiving day some Wednesday night when I didn't have time for cooking.

Dear Lord, keep me from the shortsightedness and disillusionment of the Thanksgiving guest. Let me not despair over apparent tragedy or misfortune which may be the beginning of something wonderful in Your plan. Let me ever trust in You. AMEN.

11

If you then, who are evil, know how to give good gifts to your children, how much more will your Father who is in heaven give good things to those who ask him! Matthew 7:11 (RSV)

SUCH AN AWFUL SQUAWKING! Looking out the window I saw the cause of it. A baby starling was perched on the edge of the sloping roof of the bird feeder just outside our family room. The mother bird was inside the feeder, busily pecking away at the grain we had put there. Each time the baby bird hung its head over the roof edge and squawked, the mother starling thrust some morsel of food into its open mouth.

She knew the needs of the baby bird. She was willing and able to provide for the needs of her offspring. But she couldn't feed the baby bird until he asked and prepared to receive.

Dear Lord, have You made me like the baby bird? Are there blessings You cannot give me until I ask in prayer and so prepare myself to receive them? You know my needs, better than I do. Teach me to pray, that I might receive Your blessings. AMEN.

But be doers of the word, and not hearers only, deceiving yourselves. James 1:22 (RSV)

IT WAS TIME FOR ME to renew my driver's license. I dreaded it, because, although I had no qualms about the written test, I was afraid I would fail the parallel-parking exercise if they required me to perform it under their watchful eyes.

I had studied the diagrams in the book and knew exactly how far I was supposed to be from the other car when I began to back. I knew exactly what part of my car was supposed to be opposite the bumper of the other car when I began to turn my wheels. I could recite every word of the book description of the proper method for parallel parking.

But in practice—oh, that was something entirely different! My judgement of distance and space was all wrong. I hadn't practiced the rules in an actual parking situation. Carrying them out was not an automatic part of my life behind the wheel.

Dear Lord, I confess that too often my Christianity is like my parallel parking. I know all the rules in the Book. I can quote scripture about proper Christian behavior, but I haven't made it an automatic part of my life. I haven't constantly practiced and used it. Change me, Lord, that I will not fail when the testing time comes. AMEN.

15

8

Thou dost keep him in perfect peace, whose mind is stayed on thee, because he trusts in thee. *Isaiah 26:3 (RSV)*

JAMES WAS HAVING an awful time making his bed. Tears of frustration were rolling down his cheeks when I passed his doorway and stopped to see what the trouble was. He was tugging and pulling at his brown corduroy bedspread, trying to smooth it. "It's no use!" he wailed. "It just won't get neat!"

"Well, let me have a look at it," I said as he plopped down in the middle of the floor, worn out and disgusted. "No wonder you can't get it smooth. Just look at the blanket and sheet underneath!" They were just as scrambled as they could be. His bed-making had ignored everything but the top layer.

Dear Lord, my son's foolishness about his bed-making showed me the wrinkles in my soul. I want to appear serene and calm, so I press my dress and compose my face. My efforts are futile whenever I have not taken the time to smooth my soul, by letting it be still and know that You are God. Help me, O Lord, to find my inner tranquility in You. AMEN.

17

Be still, and know that I am God. I am exalted among the nations, I am exalted in the earth! Psalms 46:10 (RSV)

BEING A GREAT PROCRASTINATOR about my mending, I find that "a stitch in time saves nine" is an understatement at my house. A stitch in time might have saved several garments that now find themselves in the ragbag, completely beyond repair.

But the old adage applies to much more than mere needle and thread mending. I remember being in a big hurry to get to my typewriter one morning. I wanted to finish some long overdue correspondence and didn't have time for my morning devotions, I thought.

The first sheet of paper I tried to insert in the typewriter got started wrong, somehow, and wound up with a torn and ruffled edge. The next one went in, all right, but I made several uneraseable errors in the inside address. Sheet number three with its carbon went in smoothly, I typed the letter without an error and pulled the sheets cheerfully from the typewriter. Then I saw that I had inserted the carbon upside down!

Such a waste of time! A very gentle reminder from my conscience suggested, "Maybe you do have time for your morning devotions, after all."

Dear Lord, in my busy life, help me to remember that I never have time to neglect You. AMEN.

. . . and lo, I am with you always, to the close of the age. Matthews 28:20 (RSV)

WE'VE INVITED A GUEST to our home for the weekend. That's why I'm doing all the extra cleaning and cooking. I want things to be especially nice, so that our guest will feel welcome.

When he comes downstairs to breakfast we'll tell him "Good morning" and that we hope he rested well. We'll talk to him at the table and see that he has some of everything good to eat—second helpings if he can hold them. I'll try to prepare all his favorite dishes.

During the day, because I know he likes to be treated like one of the family, I'll let him do things to help me. He can pick beans in the garden, oil a squeaking door and take the baby for a stroll.

At night, after supper, our guest will be the center of attention as we invite friends to come and meet him. It wouldn't occur to any of us to ignore our guest.

Oh Lord, how long has it been since I treated You as an honored guest? You are always with me, but I so seldom acknowledge Your presence. The "blessing" at the table is so perfunctory, sometimes I'm not even aware of hearing it. Halfway through the mashed potatoes someone is likely to inquire "Did anyone ask the blessing?" The answer might be, "You did. Don't you remember?" Let me start treating You like company for a change. Let me acknowledge Your presence by doing everything for Your sake. AMEN. **21**

11

And my God will supply every need of yours according to his riches in glory in Christ Jesus. Philippians 4:19 (RSV)

I READ A PRECIOUS child's letter to Santa Claus the other day. It was unselfish, for a child. She asked not just for things for herself, but listed the particular hearts' desires of her four brothers and sisters as well. The list was a long one.

Fearing that she might have overlooked something, and afraid Santa might forget a part of the list, she added a very practical P.S. "So, Santa, you might just as well bring one of everything."

Dear Lord, I think about the letter to Santa sometimes when I pray. We ask You for so many things, but may omit what we really need the most. You know our needs better than we can ever know them. Bless us according to Your wisdom and mercy with all that You want us to have. And let us use Your blessings to show forth Your glory. AMEN.

12

Lift up the light of thy countenance upon us, O Lord! Psalms 4:6 (RSV)

"SANTA CLAUS WON'T BRING you anything if you're naughty!" My friend was using her child's anticipation of the wonders of the approaching Christmas season in an attempt to chasten her willful four year old. But the four year old was not easily chastened. Standing with her feet wide apart and her hands on her diminutive hips she replied with real vehemence in her tiny voice: "Santa Claus! That's all you ever talk about—Santa Claus and Jesus Christ—and I've never seen either one of 'em!"

Telling me about the incident afterward, my friend laughed at her daughter's spunk. Then she said, seriously, "We took her to see Santa yesterday, but now she says she wants to see Jesus!"

Lord, forgive me for bearing the name of Christian without bearing the nature of Christ, so that those who know me would know Jesus. Set me about Your business of love and service so that others might see and glorify You. AMEN.

13

If thou, O Lord, shouldst mark iniquities,
Lord, who could stand? Psalms 130:3 (RSV)

EXASPERATED, the little girl's mother was wiping up the puddle of milk her daughter had deliberately poured out on the floor—to watch it splash, she said. The small daughter was rubbing her eyes crying, not so much from the spanking her mother had promptly administered as from her hurt feelings at her mother's words, "Bad girl, bad girl!"

Little Mike had watched the domestic drama with wide-eyed interest. He, too, had been shocked at his sister's mischief. But he couldn't bear to hear her cry. His mother's words, "Bad girl, bad girl!" rang in his ears. Intuitively knowing that a contradiction might not be safe at that moment, he cautiously sidled up to his sister. He patted her shoulder with a comforting hand and whispered, *"Good* bad girl, *good* bad girl."

Oh Lord, I know that I am made in Your image, to be perfect, and that You love me in spite of my sinfulness. I confess that my actions are far from the obedience to love that You require of me. Deliver me from my evil-doing, and lead me to serve Your perfect will. In Jesus' name. AMEN.

14

The true light that enlightens every man was coming into the world. John 1:9 (RSV)

It was seven o'clock on a sunshiny morning when we met a car with its bright lights still burning. How feeble and ridiculous those lights seemed by day—lights that in the darkness of the night would have been blindingly brilliant if the driver of the car had failed to dim them. By day, the lights were so dull that the driver was not even aware that they were turned on. They certainly didn't help him to see the road now, but he could not have driven without them the night before.

Dear Father in heaven, let me remember the foolish lights of that car when I am tempted to suppose that my good works could earn for me a place in heaven. Compared to Your grace, my goodness is ridiculously feeble. Give me such a constant awareness of Your presence that I will not mistake my dimness for Your light. AMEN.

15

He came for testimony, to bear witness to the light, that all might believe through him.
John 1:7 (RSV)

FOR SEVERAL YEARS I have used, with great profit and enjoyment, the lovely *Daily Study Bible* series by Dr. William Barclay. One day I loaned my copy of one of the volumes to a Sunday School classmate who wanted to use it to prepare a lesson for the following week. Returning it to me later, she expressed her thanks and explained that she had enjoyed using it. Her final comment was, "What I liked most about it is that Dr. Barclay's old-fashioned, kind of. You know, he talks about God as if it's true."

Oh Lord, I thank You for the witness of the scholarship of men like Dr. Barclay who know that You are real in their lives. Use me and the witness of my tongue and pen and life to convey to those about me the trueness, the awesome realness and aliveness of You. Let me more perfectly love You through Jesus Christ, our Lord. AMEN.

16

Come to me, all who labor and are heavy laden, and I will give you rest. Matthew 11:28 (RSV)

SUCH CONTORTIONS! Susan, my middle daughter, was getting ready for bed, with her hands flying frantically trying to scratch every part of her frame. "Mama, I just itch terrible all over!" she wailed. She and some of her little playmates had been having a grass fight in the side yard.

Knowing a bath would be wonderfully soothing to her distress, I suggested, "Well, then, let's have you hop in the tub before you go to bed."

Her reply was immediate and quite negative. Apparently she had already considered such a move and had rejected it. "No," she complained, still wriggling, "I'd rather just scratch, 'cause I don't want to have to take my pajamas off and put them on again."

Dear Lord, how often I am too lazy to take my problems to You for Your healing. Like Susan, I think I would rather bear my miseries than receive the perfect peace You alone can give. Change me now, give me such an awareness of Your presence and Your loveliness that nothing can keep me from seeking You. AMEN.

17

As the Lord has forgiven you, so you also must forgive. Colossians 3:13 (RSV)

"I'LL NEVER FORGET it as long as I live!" That expression has the ring of familiarity to me that could only have come from my having said it on numerous occasions. I remember few of the joyful situations which prompted it. But it is easy for me to remember the unpleasant ones.

Real or imagined slights or insults that have come to me can be dredged up out of my memory with all the details magnified by time. Indignation and hostility are born again out of something I thought I had forgiven long ago. My forgetter seems to work best when there is nothing to forgive.

Dear Lord, I confess to being afraid sometimes when I pray, "Forgive us our trespasses as we forgive those who trespass against us." My forgiving is so short-lived, so superficial, so false. I have to forgive seventy times seven for a single trivial offense. Teach me perfect forgetting, which is perfect forgiveness, that I may inherit Your kingdom. AMEN.

18

Let brotherly love continue. Do not neglect to show hospitality to strangers, for thereby some have entertained angels unawares. Hebrews 13:1, 2 (RSV)

CHRISTMAS TREES ARE beautiful, but, like many another housewife I know, I'm glad to sweep out the dropped needles and untrim the tree when the holidays are over. I'm glad to be done with it—all the lovely, but hectic, holiday activities—so that we can get back to normal living. Back to normal means, in part, that instant hospitality and cordial greetings to many friends are over until the next holiday season rolls around. And, if my brisk actions do not belie my thoughts, it's as if, on cleaning-up day, I pledge myself to have no time for the nonsense of friendship or the courtesy of charity. I'm getting "straightened around" again.

Oh Lord, forgive me if I have swept out my good will toward men, the reflection of Your love, along with the tarnished tinsel and the broken ornaments and the burned out bulbs. Let me keep Christmas in my heart all the year round, so that those who come to my house will know that You dwell here, and that the Christ Child is born anew each day in my heart. AMEN.

19

Let the children come to me, and do not hinder them; for to such belongs the kingdom of God. Luke 18:16 (RSV)

BECAUSE THE DOCTOR had predicted that our new baby would arrive on the Tuesday before Thanksgiving I had not invited any dinner guests for Thanksgiving turkey. I knew that "turkey" might be a can of soup opened by an unaccustomed cook while I was in the hospital. As it happened, the baby delayed her appearance for some weeks and I was at home with just my family for Thanksgiving Day. I missed the sharing that had been such an important part of our Thanksgiving in other years. But I enjoyed our children that day and paid real attention to them as we all went for a walk in the woods.

Oh Lord, let me continue to be hospitable to Your children, everywhere. But let me use some special times, when circumstances require our aloneness as a family, when I may be with my own children in loving, unhurried ways, when I can listen to them instead of shush them for the important talk of grownup company. AMEN.

20

In those times there was no peace to him who went out or to him who came in, for great disturbances afflicted all the inhabitants of the lands. 2 Chronicles 15:5 (RSV)

You are anxious and troubled about many things. One thing is needful. Luke 10:41, 42 (RSV)

It couldn't have been a man whose wife was in the throes of spring housecleaning who said, "Cleanliness is next to godliness." Burdened with backbreaking chores of furniture moving after a hard day at the office a man might think that cleanliness was the work of the devil. And he'd have been right.

The way I go about putting my house in order sometimes bears very little relationship to anything having remotely to do with heaven. Over-meticulous housekeeping females—on the warpath against every speck of dirt, stray hairpin, open book, stamp collection clutter, soggy box of clay for Neanderthal pottery—destroy creativity and happiness in the husband and children who have to put up with them.

Dear Lord, I thank You for the days when my hormones are in the kind of balance that lets me tolerate the messiness of living in our home. Let not my passion for orderliness on other days destroy the peace of those about me. Give me moderation in the things appropriate to it, and fanatical devotion only to You. AMEN.

21

Thou dost keep him in perfect peace, whose mind is stayed on thee, because he trusts in thee. Isaiah 26:3 (RSV)

OVERWEIGHT IS A widespread health problem in America. It is my problem too. Periodically I think about my need to lose ten pounds or so and resolve to do something about it. Often, on days when I think about dieting—usually after a more than adequate meal—I get an almost immediate headache from gritting my teeth over not-eating while my thoughts are stayed on food. Then, of course, I can justify a snack along with an aspirin to cure my headache. That doesn't help my weight problem much.

Neither do misguided housecleaning moods when I clear out all the interesting little dabs of leftovers in the refrigerator by eating them. It may leave the refrigerator in good shape, but oh, what it does to the shape of me! Concern with my problem keeps me defeated.

Oh Lord, deliver me from the foolishness of preoccupation with any of my problems or shortcomings. Give me the grace to follow a path of attention to You and so receive Your healing and forgiving grace in all things. AMEN.

43

22

And calling to him a child, he put him in the midst of them, and said, "Truly, I say to you, unless you turn and become like children, you will never enter the kingdom of heaven." Matthew 18:2, 3 (RSV)

IT WAS A BEAUTIFUL, breezy, warm day when I took baby for a stroll. Even I could appreciate the special loveliness of the weather. But baby enjoyed the day in a different way. She laughed the whole way around the block, tickled with delight at the way the breeze was blowing her hair. She acted as if she thought the breeze was invented deliberately for her own personal pleasure. She was as responsive to every bit of breeze as if she could actually see some person blowing at her to make her happy.

Let me take all Your blessings of beauty—and sacrifice— personally. Let me fully enjoy the loveliness of Your creation. Let me think of Jesus as one who died for me. May I live in the light and confidence of that belief. AMEN.

And let us not grow weary in well-doing, for in due season we shall reap, if we do not lose heart. Galatians 6:9 (RSV)

Running a servantless household has many compensations. For one thing, I am the one to discover and retrieve things that fall to the floor when I pull a bed away from the wall on sheet-washing day. One morning something small clicked onto the floor as I moved the boys' bunk beds. Stooping to pick up the small matchbox I was annoyed at first. The boys know they're not supposed to have matches, I fumed, resolved to scold them when they got home from school. My annoyance changed to worry when I opened the box and saw that all the matches had been struck. The box held only the carefully preserved charred fragments of the fragile, burned matchsticks. Mercy! They could have set the house on fire, playing with matches in bed.

A wave of despondency, a realization of failure, swept sickeningly over me as I thought of all the times I had told them that fire was not for playing with. But then a further thought arose. I had told them, "No," all right, but had I given them sufficient opportunities to light fires in the fireplace or burn trash outdoors under carefully supervised conditions? Had I let them satisfy their natural curiosities safely about burning matches? I had to admit the answer to that was "No."

Oh Lord, keep me from discouragement at my failures, when, compared to Your sacrifice for erring men, I have not even begun to try. Let me know that my only success is from You and in You. In Jesus' name. AMEN.

47

24

You see that faith was active along with his works, and faith was completed by works.
James 2:22 (RSV)

A MEMBER OF A civic organization knocked on my door the other night to ask me to buy a new broom. I buy brooms from the same "benefit the blind" drive every year, usually not before I need to replace a shedding, lopsided, worn-out, unsatisfactory old one.

I don't quite hold to the old adage "A new broom sweeps clean." It seems to me that a new broom is usually very stiff and hard to use to get dirt off the floor. But, compared to the poor excuse I had been trying to use, the new broom did quite well at that. From my past experience I knew that the new broom just needed a little practice and breaking in to be very serviceable.

Oh Lord, my faith in You is like a new broom. It doesn't work very well for me unless I make it supple with constant use. Let me keep my faith broken in so that it can render good service for men and for You in faithful witness to those about me. AMEN.

25

We know that in everything God works for good with those who love him, who are called according to his purpose. Romans 8:28 (RSV)

We had room for a garden at the back of the lot of our new house. But the soil didn't look good. It was clay baked hard when the weather was dry and a running gluey mess when a rain had fallen on it. It wasn't much good for raising anything except a cloud of dust when the wind hit it in a dry spell.

But my husband, an organic gardener, began to work on it. He took the refuse from the kitchen, the sweepings from the yard and street, the waste from a cotton gin and a peanut warehouse—the leavings, the garbage of their industries and mine—and buried them where God could turn them into soil. No waste was too unpleasant to use. Several times I worried that his enthusiasm for composting might lead him to ask the neighbors for their garbage. Well, he never did that, but he doesn't deny that he wanted to, many times.

Today, just five years later, the freezer is full of the garden's summer bounty. We've fed our family and friends all they could hold. I should be canning more tomatoes this afternoon. We've a fall garden going full swing. The garden soil is loose and rich, full of organic matter, prospering the growth of anything he plants there. The enriching materials have been only a few loads of "boughten" nutrients but all the garbage and trash he could scrap together.

Let me, Oh Lord, not despair of making something out of the barren places of my life. Teach me to use my mistakes and failures, the garbage of my life, to witness to You and to make my life fruitful in Your service. Amen.

51

26

May the God of hope fill you with all joy and peace in believing, so that by the power of the Holy Spirit you may abound in hope.
Romans 15:13 (RSV)

THE ELDERLY woman who came to have lunch with us was unexpected, but welcome. Only she wasn't able to eat much that I had put on the table. Thirty years earlier she had had all of her teeth extracted. At that time, believing herself to be an old woman already, she couldn't see the sense of spending money to buy an upper and a lower plate for chewing. She had no hope that she would live long enough to make the expenditure worthwhile. That was why she bought only a lower plate. Half a set of store teeth wasn't much better than none at all. So Miss Martha has been gumming her food for thirty years.

Dear Lord, keep me from thinking it is ever too late to serve You. Keep me from thinking it isn't worth beginning because I am already as old as I am, or as weak, or as sunk in wrongdoing. It can't ever be too late to try, with You on my side. Let me serve You this day. AMEN.

27

By much slothfulness the building decayeth; and through idleness of the hands the house droppeth through. Ecclesiastes 10:18 (KJV)

ONE DAY WHEN the children were small I was appalled to see a pile of silky brown hair in the middle of the girls' bedroom floor. I was half afraid to look at my youngest daughter. When I did, I had to bury my face in my hands and cry a little before I could ask the question. My child's beautiful hair looked like a scarecrow's—all bristly and lopped off in uneven lengths.

"Susan, who did it?"

"I did it, Mama," my usually unmischievous Alice admitted.

I couldn't understand it. "Alice," I asked, "why whatever got into you?" I was more surprised than angry at my responsible and trustworthy child.

"Well, Mama," she explained in a manner that showed her remorseful but helpless, "I didn't have anything else to do."

Oh Lord, I too do things I should not. Forgive me for my idleness—the times I have not been attuned to You. Keep me so busy at Your business, serving You, that I don't have time to get into trouble. I ask in Jesus' name. AMEN. **55**

28

Take my yoke upon you, and learn from me; for I am gentle and lowly in heart, and you will find rest for your souls. For my yoke is easy, and my burden is light. Matthew 11: 29, 30 (RSV)

ALICE HAD OUTGROWN her petticoat. Fortunately it was a type with a built-in grow-tuck around the waist. The stitching was supposed to unravel effortlessly when you pulled the right thread. How I labored trying to get the right one. From my point of beginning I tried every thread from every angle. Each inch was a laborious, tedious, razoring job.

Then it occurred to me that I might be heading in the wrong direction. Going back to the other edge of the beginning gap, I gently tugged at a protruding thread. The whole tuck fell open as if by magic.

Oh Lord, how many times a day I find myself doing something the hard way because it hasn't occurred to me that I might be headed in the wrong direction. Turn me about. Let my mistakes in this little thing be a constant reminder that in all things only Your way is the right way for my life. To try to go against You is to waste time, to frustrate myself, and fail to fulfill Your purpose for my life. Lead me in Your perfect will. AMEN.

29

For we are fellow workmen for God. 1 Corinthians 3:9 (RSV)

"I JUST HATE dirty dishes!" My daughter's vehemence as she began to clear off the supper table was almost funny. Since I was busy ironing her Girl Scout uniform I knew she wasn't asking me for help in this outburst. She was just saying what she felt.

I'm not usually in love with dirty dishes, either, and I watched her as she tackled the job to be done. To my surprise she didn't break any in her handling of them and they were all washed, dried and put away in short order.

"There!" she exclaimed with a satisfied smile as she shut the last cupboard door.

"Finished my uniform yet, Mom?" she asked.

As I handed it to her I mentioned her outburst and asked, "What's the best thing to do with dirty dishes you hate, Alice?"

She got the point almost before I finished the question.

"I know," she twinkled back at me, "turn 'em into clean ones."

Help me not to turn my back on the things I hate for Your sake. Help me face them and, with Your help, change their ugliness into loveliness, worthy of Your love. AMEN. **59**

30

A faithful man will abound with blessings.
Proverbs 28:20 (RSV)

My HUSBAND and the boys are at work building bluebird boxes. They've measured carefully, following instructions in the encyclopedia for just the kind of house bluebirds prefer. When they've finished their carpentry they'll nail the houses up and we'll all watch for the birds. Some of our friends are building bluebird houses too.

The strange thing about it is that none of us has seen a bluebird in this part of the country for more than ten years. But we have faith in the knowledge of the ornithologist who assures us that bluebirds will come when the houses are available for them.

Oh Lord, we look for bluebirds in vain until we are prepared to receive them. We have to believe in bluebirds enough to get ready for them before they come. Give me the same kind of faith in Your grace. Give me the obedience to daily reading of the Bible, to daily prayer to You, and to continual awareness of Your presence, that I may receive Your grace. I know You have already given it. Let me receive it and use it to Your glory. AMEN.

31

Lay not up for yourselves treasures upon earth, where moth and rust doth corrupt, and where thieves break through and steal; but lay up for yourselves treasures in heaven, where neither moth nor rust doth corrupt, and where thieves do not break through nor steal; For where your treasure is, there will your heart be also. Matthew 6:19-21 (KJV)

THE OTHER DAY I read a newspaper account about a scientist who had arranged to have his body frozen after his death and buried in Alaska. There he plans to remain frozen for five hundred years. At that time he is certain science will have found a cure for whatever caused his death and will be able to thaw him out and restore him to life.

I shivered when I read about it—a chilling prospect, to say the least.

What if he has a deathbed conversion with no opportunity to change his will? And then, five hundred years later his soul, radiant in heaven, is dragged back to inhabit his revived, but decrepit body? What then? That's a chillier prospect still.

Lord, often I am just as foolish and unfaithful as the scientist. I place my faith in worldly things. Help me believe and live in Your promise of eternal life, not limited by this earthly body with its aches and pains, but in a new being, clothed in Your glory. In Jesus' name. AMEN.

32

I must work the works of him that sent me, while it is day: the night cometh when no man can work. John 9:4 (KJV)

IT WAS BEDTIME and Tommy had not finished his homework. He had spent two hours, when he was supposed to be studying, reading a book instead. Confronted with his failure to be dependable he complained, "My conscience just didn't make me get busy. It doesn't work good enough."

Dear Lord, my conscience isn't working too well either. When I look back at my failure to do unto the least of these as I would want to have done unto You, I can see it. Keep my mind so on You that my conscience, the working of Your Holy Spirit in me, will not go unheeded and let me fail to do my duty. Let me not come to judgement with my homework unfinished. In Jesus' name I pray. AMEN.

Who art thou that judgest another man's servant? to his own master he standeth or falleth. Romans 14:4 (KJV)

IN OUR ATTEMPTS to help other people we sometimes make a wrong diagnosis of the problem. That happened to the Judge the other day as he sat on the bench.

A man, who had not been getting along with his wife, was being tried for public drunkenness. The Judge had to find him guilty and, since the man was already on probation, sentence him to prison.

The small wiry husband and the grossly fat wife embraced in a tearful goodbye, their marital discord temporarily forgotten in the pain of separation. Later the Judge listened to the prisoner's account of his presently unhappy marriage. Sure that one of the basic difficulties was his wife's gargantuan size, the Judge could not resist a question.

"Tell me," he asked gently and sympathetically, "was she that big when you married her?"

"That big?" The prisoner opened his eyes in wide indignation. "That big? Why, Your Honor, she's fallen off forty pounds! She only weighs 190 now—weighed 'round 230 when I married her. I like my women big!"

I don't think the Judge had anything else to say.

Oh Lord, lead me not to judge others. Lead me not to criticize them for shortcomings, but let me live so close to You that they will be drawn nearer to Your peace. AMEN. **67**

34

For God so loved the world, that he gave his only begotten Son, that whosoever believeth in him should not perish, but have everlasting life. John 3:16 (KJV)

It was just a few days until Christmas. After the children were asleep my husband and I were discussing the shopping we'd done and what things still needed to be purchased for family and friends. It all added up to too much money and we knew it. Our budget would be strained for months.

"Well, what's done is done," I said to him. "One thing's sure, if we counted the cost of Christmas to begin with we'd never have the nerve to go through with it."

Oh my God, forgive me for thinking that the cost of Christmas could be measured in dollars spent at the store. If You had counted the cost of Christmas—the cost, the unbearable burden, of sending You Son to earth as a tiny babe to be mocked, scourged and crucified—could You have done it? And yet, knowing all things, You did.

Let me remember the real cost of Christmas. Be so in my mind and heart that I cannot be selfish or stingy or counting the cost of my small kindnesses to others in Your name. Let me wholly accept Your gift for my salvation and not waste it. Amen.

69

35

Cause me to hear thy lovingkindness in the morning; for in thee do I trust: cause me to know the way wherein I should walk; for I lift up my soul unto thee. Psalms 143:8 (KJV)

I HAVE BEEN helping to teach a deaf child. When I want to tell her something I have to get her attention on my face. She has to look at my lips in order to read there what I want her to know. Without her attention fixed on me I can talk and talk, as if I were telling her many things, to no avail. Not only does she not understand what I am saying, she does not even know that I am saying anything. She has to learn to listen with all her senses. Only with her complete attention—her eyes on my face and her hands on my throat—can she "hear" what I say.

Oh Lord, I am like a deaf child. I cannot hear You unless I turn my attention to You. Have You been telling me something about Your will for me and I have not known it, have not even acknowledged You were speaking to me, much less comprehended Your message? Turn my heart and soul and mind so to You that I cannot fail to understand what You would have me know. Focus me in Your direction, away from the myriad ways of the world. AMEN.

36

*Strait is the gate, and narrow is the way,
which leadeth unto life. Matthew 7:14 (KJV)*

POWER HAS TAKEN over our lives. Everything is automated. That's convenient, but there are perils in power. A slight effort from us, almost negligible as far as its drain on our physical energies is concerned, sets into motion far-reaching results.

Take power steering in my automobile, for instance. With effortless ease I might go cavorting in circles in the middle of Main Street when all I meant to do was to swerve two inches to the left to avoid an open manhole. Or on the freeway. If I don't watch it, I'll commit to irreversible action a moment's indecision or bad judgment. I can't afford to make a mistake. When I know I've made one anyhow, I can't slow down and prepare to get off. I have to stay in the flow of traffic, going at its rate until an opportunity to turn finally presents itself. That may not be for miles, after I've gone a great distance out of my way. All this is why I let my husband do most of the driving these days.

Oh Lord, in my spiritual life too, a slight touch can make all the difference. A mistaken turn in the wrong direction sometimes carries me far out of Your way. Make me mindful of and obedient to Your road signs that I may keep on the course. Let Your power for good work in me. AMEN.   **73**

37

Blessed be ye poor: for yours is the kingdom of God. Luke 6:20 (KJV)

A VIVID NEWSPAPER account of a kidnapping had my eight year old daughter worried. She didn't want to go upstairs to bed.

"What if someone gets on a ladder and comes in the window to kidnap me?" she asked tearfully.

We comforted her as best we could and explained that we were going to be right there, downstairs. That explanation didn't satisfy her so we added another.

"Besides," we explained, "kidnappers wouldn't be interested in you unless we had a lot of money to pay them for your safe return—unless we were very rich."

Susan knew something of our budgetary problems so that sounded promising, but there was another question.

"Well, how will they know we're not rich?" she asked.

We named some of the things we didn't have, things that were usually present as symbols of affluence where it existed. We had no TV, no second car, no diamonds, no motor boats, no mink coats, no yachts. Our house was not elaborate or fine. There were no servants. Susan caught on cheerfully and named a few other things we did not have that some of her playmates did.

"I sure am glad we're poor," she said, finally, kissed us goodnight and went up to bed and to untroubled sleep.

My Lord, how much I learn when I try to teach Your children. Let me see the blessings of earthly poverty, the peace of the true knowledge and seeking after You. Let me not permit the temptations of the world to take me from Your side. AMEN.

38

He hath made everything beautiful in his time. Ecclesiastes 3:11 (KJV)

ONE OF MY CHILDREN had a new teacher whom I'd never met. He had tried to tell me about her, saying, "Well, I don't know how to describe her exactly—but she's real purty!"

A few days later my daughter pointed his teacher out to me across a department store. The woman I saw was of average height and weight. Her face was far from what I'd call "pretty." Well, I thought, he must really like her.

At the first PTA meeting of the year I met my son's new teacher and heard her explain to parents how she always begins the school day with a devotional and a prayer.

"The day always seems to go better if we ask for His help at the beginning," she said.

After the orientation session I introduced myself and told her, "My boy's enjoying you so much!"

"Oh, I'm enjoying him, too," she exclaimed. "He's so smart, why he's one of my very best readers. Did you see the picture he drew for us? I've put it on the bulletin board."

Why, I thought, she's as proud of him as if he were her own little boy! By the time I left the room I had new respect for my son's taste in women. His teacher is truly "real purty."

Oh Lord, forgive me when I judge beauty by externals. Let me remember this teacher and all others whom I've considered unbeautiful before I came close to their lives and found You shining through them. Help me to see the beauty in all I encounter in my life's pathway. And, for myself, let me not be concerned unduly with the external things of my appearance, but with the tending of that "inner light" which can glow through the plainest of faces and make them beautiful to behold. AMEN.

77

39

But my God shall supply all your need according to his riches in glory by Christ Jesus.
Philippians 4:19 (KJV)

For Sale. The ad described exactly the kind of house we'd been looking for. I called the real estate man and made an early appointment to go look at it. Tulips were blooming bright red against the snowy paint of the white clapboards. A low porch invited us in. We were charmed. This was the house for us.

The next week I hired a baby sitter and went back to work full time so that we could afford to make the payments. I had already begun to pack books and china to move to the new house.

And then our plans were shattered. With our still limited financial resources we needed someone to take a second mortgage on the house. No one was willing. Special financial arrangements we had hoped to work out with the builder-contractor could not be made.

Someone else bought "our house." I unpacked the books and china and put them back on the old, crowded shelves. At first we were so disappointed.

But within a year we had begun to build our "dream home." It was on a perfect lot, conveniently located. The children could walk to school without crossing a street, my husband could bicycle uptown to his office and my job was a brief twenty minute walk from the breakfast table. And financing was no problem at all.

Dear Lord, how often what seems to us adversity is really something working for our good. It has happened so often in my life that sometimes, in the midst of what seems disappointment, I am tempted to stop and ask, "What very special thing is God planning for us instead?"

I thank You for Your goodness. Let me always have faith that Your purpose will be worked out in our lives. Amen. **79**

40

A little child lead them. Isaiah 11:6 (KJV)

ALL OF A SUDDEN Marie missed her little boy. He had been standing to one side, waiting while she said good-bye to the children going home from her Sunday School class.

"Bobby, where are you?" she called.

"I'm here, Mama, behind the door," a small voice answered.

Looking behind the door, Marie saw her child standing, with his eyes closed, his lips moving soundlessly, his hands tucked under his little chin in an attitude of prayer. She waited 'til he came out before she asked, "What were you doing that for, Bobby?"

"Well, Mama," he explained, "I could see that you were busy and I didn't want to waste my time so I thought I'd just pray God a little prayer."

Dear Lord, forgive me for not being more like Bobby. I often find myself fretting over wasted time when I'm waiting for someone. Teach me to use all my waiting moments in waiting on You, in praying peacegiving prayers. AMEN.

41

And he that sat upon the throne said, Behold, I make all things new. And he said unto me, Write: for these words are true and faithful. Revelation 21:5 (KJV)

TODAY I FINISHED reading a devotional book which has been a part of my daily "quiet time" for several weeks. *The Private Devotions of Lancelot Andrewes*—how much it has added to my private devotions! How lifted up it has left me!

I am sure that, for me, the Scripture "For where two or three are gathered together in my name, there am I in the midst of them" (Matthew 18:20) can be interpreted to allow Lancelot Andrewes and myself to be two gathered in His name, even though Lancelot Andrewes died more than three hundred years ago.

Dear Lord, I thank You for books; for money to buy them; for friends and libraries from which to borrow them; for time and ability to read them; for the authors who were able to receive Your graces of diligence and devotion and inspiration to write them; for mind to understand them and soul to profit from their reading.

All these and other things good in my life I acknowledge as precious gifts from You, not of my doing. Stay in my awareness forever as You are at this moment and live in my life so men will know You. AMEN.

42

For your Father knoweth what things ye have need of, before ye ask him. Matthew 6:8 (KJV)

MORE THAN ANYTHING else, Monnica, the mother of the young man who was to become St. Augustine, wanted her son to become a member of the Church. She shed many tears and prayed many prayers to that end, seemingly to no avail. Augustine went from one heresy to another and lived an immoral life.

When Augustine decided to sail for Milan to get a job as a teacher, Monnica begged him not to go. She could not accompany him and felt that away from her influence he would stray even further from the truth. Her tears and pleadings wrung from Augustine a promise that he would not leave her.

Upon the pretense of telling a friend good-bye, Augustine left his trusting mother and sneaked away in the night. In the morning she learned that he had sailed. Her heart was broken.

In Milan, however, Augustine came under the influence of the Bishop Ambrose whose teaching began to turn Augustine to God. The very voyage that Augustine's mother had prayed he would not make brought him closer to God and closer to the answer to her real prayers.

Lord, let me pray "Thy will be done," aware You know our needs. Let me trust in Your mercy and wisdom and lovingkindness for all Your children. In Jesus' name. AMEN.   **85**

43

Verily I say unto you, Inasmuch as ye did it not to one of the least of these, ye did it not to me. Matthew 25:45 (KJV)

"How ON EARTH do you do it all, Irene?"

My friend asked me the question with real puzzlement in her eyes. When I attempted to turn it off with a dissembling, "Oh, I don't do so much," she insisted, "No, really, here you are with a full time job, a house full of children, no household help, you teach Sunday school, cook for lots of company and still find time to write. I just want to know how you do it."

I had been asked the same question before and had always supposed that I found extra time by being efficient in my housework, by not belonging to clubs, or by not playing bridge or golf. Sometimes I gave a little credit to my husband who was good about picking up groceries and dry cleaning and wearing wrinkled suits and unstarched shirts. And I boasted relatively low housekeeping standards that kept my waxing of furniture and floors infrequent and my window washing almost non-existent. But usually I took most of the credit for myself with a hypocritical demurrer, "Oh, I don't do so much, really."

But these answers didn't satisfy even me this time. My friend also worked, had no household help, had several children and never seemed to waste time. She was forever doing things for other people—for her friends. I never found time for much of that.

Thinking about her life and the lovely witness of it I had a painfully honest answer to her question. "It's so easy to find the time, Ruth," I said. "All you have to do is neglect your friends. That's where I find the time."

Dear Lord, forgive me that I have failed to cherish the friends You have given me. I let them do so much for me, but I don't even go to see them. Take the vanity of worldly accomplishment from me and send me out to minister to Your children. Make the realization of my sin the beginning of my healing from it. I ask in Jesus' name. AMEN.

44

For they verily for a few days chastened us after their own pleasure; but he for our profit, that we might be partakers of his holiness. Hebrews 12:10 (KJV)

As soon as the barest hint of fall was in the air my husband struck a match to the kindling in our new fireplace. The rest of us heaved contented sighs and settled back to enjoy an evening before the fire. In a few minutes we were dashing about opening doors and windows instead to fan out the billows of smoke that burned our eyes and blackened the ceiling.

After weeks of smoking fires we learned the difficulty. The fireplace opening was too big for the size of the flue.

After we told our contractor he sent his brick mason to install two rows of bricks at the top of the fireplace opening to correct the problem. The remedy was effective.

When the itemized repair bill came I was reluctant to pay all of it. I didn't mind paying for materials and labor but one item was listed as "contractor's profit." I didn't see why he should profit from his mistake!

Oh Lord, is there anything that cannot teach us how to serve You? I, too, profit from my mistakes—many of which are more painful to other people than to me. Let me not condemn another for doing the same thing when I am so far from Your perfection. Chasten me to my profit and Your glory. AMEN.

45

But to all who received him, who believed in his name, he gave power to become children of God. John 1:12 (RSV)

GROWN-UP VISITORS frequently ask our four older children, "What are you going to be when you grow up?" Their answers have varied from year to year, and have included almost everything from aviator to zoologist. The answer I remember best is the one Susan gave when she was four years old. The visitor had begun with the oldest child and found out that we had one potential pilot, one school teacher and one baby doctor. Then he came to Susan. She didn't have to think at all. She looked up and smiled and said, "I'm just gonna be what I am!"

For Susan that was a wonderfully happy answer—a lovely future is in store for her if she can continue to be like she is, knowing without any doubt that Jesus loves her, and responding by loving all about her. For some of the rest of us to know that we would continue to be what we are would be a terrible sentence.

Oh Lord, I am so far from what I ought to be. Created in Your image, I have not lived a life that reflected You. My heavenly Father, give me the grace to choose to be Yours, to grow up into the fullness of Your promise. AMEN.

(Appeared first, slightly revised, in *Power* for Oct.-Nov.-Dec., 1965.)

46

But seek first his kingdom and his righteous-
ness, and all these things shall be yours as well.
Matthew 6:33 (RSV)

FIVE YEAR OLD Betty was spending the day with her grandmother who keeps a small country store. Betty waited on some of the small customers herself, especially the little boys who came in with a few pennies for candy.

Her grandmother watched her help one young man. Betty tried to sell him some of her favorite kind of candy, but he had his heart set on another variety instead. All of her recommendations could not change his mind.

Finally Betty stomped her little foot in exasperation and said, "Well, all right then! You can have what you want! But that other's the best!"

Oh God, I know that You intend the very best for all of Your children. And, all wise, You tell us to seek first Your kingdom and Your righteousness. Forgive me that I so often act as if I think I know best, and choose the wrong way, failing to heed Your call.

Let me use my freedom to choose Your way, and receive Your blessing. Help me to know that in seeking You I choose the highest good for my life. AMEN.

(Appeared first, slightly revised, in *Power* for Oct.-Nov.-Dec., 1965.)

47

It is not the will of your Father which is in heaven, that one of these little ones should perish. Matthew 18:14 (KJV)

THIS MORNING THE bananas in the fruit bowl were just ripe-right for making bread. Tomorrow they'd have been too soft. So I took the time to sift and stir, and now a special fragrance fills the air. Soon I'll take from the oven loaves that are high and light and crusty-brown—substantial fare the children will enjoy with salty butter and cold glasses of milk when they troop home from school.

If I had waited until tomorrow the bananas would have been garbage instead. My opportunity would have been gone to turn something fleeting into more lasting good.

Oh Lord, I know a few wasted bananas wouldn't matter much. But wasted opportunities to serve You matter a lot. And I waste so many. Forgive me. Let me recognize and fulfill every opportunity this day, before it's too late, for the love of Him who died for us all. AMEN.

48

And a little child shall lead them. Isaiah 11:6 (KJV)

First-Born

Awake, I hear across the hall
A "gup-gup-gup" and, tempted, look
To see a small head peep at me
And then turn, bashful in delight,
To hide his sweet, sweet smile.

All the day the sounds are there:
Nipple-noises singing,
Contented grunts accompanying,
As baby drains his sustenance;
The rowdiness of bottle thrown
Out of the crib to watch it fall;
And baas and squeaks and jingles
Of toys he shakes or sits on.
Discontent, and "Muh-muh-muh"—
Oh, how it thrills!
But does he know it has a sense
Beyond his small tongue's exercise?

And that same small head, fighting sleep,
But still rooting on my shoulder
For a place a head can rest—
The day ends to a lullaby
Of rocker springs.

These are things
Of my Thanksgiving.

*Oh Lord, I thank You for the precious gift of a child to
love and care for. Let him keep me ever mindful of You
in the joys he brings to my life.* AMEN.   **97**

49

Bless the Lord, O my soul, and forget not all his benefits. Psalms 103:2 (KJV)

Inventory

For other blessings,
I pray God not;
But let me thank Him
For those I've got.

Dear Father in heaven, I know that all the good things in my life are gifts from You. And there are so many more good things than I think to acknowledge in the midst of my complaints and petitions. This day, let me be properly aware of, and sincerely thankful for, Your many blessings to me— especially for the incomparable blessing of eternal life through Jesus Christ, my Lord. In His name I pray. AMEN.

50

Then let us no more pass judgment on one another, but rather decide never to put a stumbling-block or hindrance in the way of a brother. Romans 14:13 (RSV)

Confession

There are blind who cannot see:
Lay them to me, Lord, lay them to me
Where I have seen thy glory
And not reflected thy love.

There are deaf who cannot hear:
Lay them to me, Lord, lay them to me
Where I have heard thy voice
And have not sung thy praise.

There are lame who cannot walk:
Lay them to me, Lord, lay them to me
Where I have known thy way
And been a stumbling block.

Precious Lord, who bearest all of the burden for all of my guilt, all of the grief for all of my shame, cleanse me this day and make me wholly Thine. Let me not keep heaven from earth with sins of self. In Jesus' name I pray. Amen. **101**